Karen wait
while Carl a
They were g
whether sh
not—things
lately. But maybe dinner and a movie
would take her mind off their son's
belligerent behavior . . . and the deep
lurking feeling that something was
desperately wrong.

Then she heard Carl lower his
voice. "I told you never to call me at
home. What *is* it?"

A moment later Carl was by her side
with her coat. As she slipped her arm
into the sleeve, their eyes met and
locked.

"Karen," he blurted, "I love her."

Carl and Karen had a marriage which seemed
"perfect." But long before the affair, unspoken
choices were made that led to what seemed to
be the sudden breakup of a perfect marriage.

Every marriage has seeds for growth and seeds
for destruction. All marriages have problems. As
you read the true stories in this book, you'll learn
how to recognize seeds that can produce destruction, and how these same problems can become
seeds of personal and marital growth.

When It's Hard to Trust

STEVE WILKE
DAVE & NETA JACKSON

LIVING BOOKS®
Tyndale House Publishers, Inc.
Wheaton, Illinois

Living Books is a registered trademark of Tyndale House Publishers, Inc.

Library of Congress Catalog Card Number 91-75029
ISBN 0-8423-7955-X
© 1991 by Stephen K. Wilke and Dave and Neta Jackson
Printed in the United States of America

98   97   96   95   94   93
8   7   6   5   4

CONTENTS

Introduction

Affairs are seldom as simple and never so glamorous as they appear in the movies. Few married people fall for the charmer at the office without a whole lot of history leading up to the liaison. That history may include some seemingly innocent flirtation, and there can be real danger in that.

For instance, several years ago, I (Dave Jackson) traveled across the country with several others from our church to a leadership conference. Our return was on a half-filled night train, and many of us had managed to claim two seats apiece in which to spread out. But at one o'clock in the morning, when we rolled quietly into Kansas City, dim lights came on to help new passengers find places.

An attractive woman made her way down the aisle with her bags, looking from side to side for someone to move. I turned toward the window and watched her in the reflection.

"May I sit here?" she asked.

"Oh, yeah, sure." I looked up and

smiled as I moved over. She threw her things into the rack above and sat down. Near the back of the car, only one of my colleagues had managed to keep his extra space. Lucky guy.

"My name's Kathy. What's yours?"

I told her, and we talked quietly for a while. She was on her way to visit her mother after some rough spats with her husband. I was anxious to get home and see my wife and family after an exhausting conference.

Soon we both slipped off to sleep. At some later stop I awoke to find Kathy cuddled over next to me. "You don't mind if I lean my head on your shoulder, do you?" she said sleepily.

"Uh, no. I guess not." She was just tired . . . wasn't she? And besides, I had a wonderful wife and marriage and would be home before noon. I looked around to see if anyone was noticing.

She cuddled closer. I wondered what she really wanted—or would allow. At first I couldn't believe what I was thinking. But then it *was* her fault. She knew exactly what she was doing. I might as well enjoy it. After all, what could happen on a train full of people? Nothing, nothing really, except what Jesus warned about happening in the heart: imagining an illicit affair.

Finally, I got up and went back to sit with my friend—the "lucky" one with the extra seat beside him. Or maybe *I* was the lucky one since that extra space was still available. All I knew was that I hadn't been making it where I had been.

And perhaps it wasn't luck at all. Maybe it was the "way to escape" that the Bible promises will always be available when we are tempted (1 Corinthians 10:13).

We have all been shocked in recent years by reports of the sexual misconduct of certain prominent religious leaders. Their hypocrisy may disgust us, and rightly so. But sex is a powerful force. When *Christianity Today* magazine polled one thousand of its subscribers—presumably "good Christian people"—it discovered that 23 percent said they had had extramarital intercourse, and 28 percent said they had engaged in other forms of extramarital sexual contact.[1]

So, if this tragedy has smashed into your life, you at least are not alone or unusual.

Jerry Jenkins, in his book, *Hedges: Loving Your Marriage Enough to Protect It*, says, "Scripture does not imply that we ever shall have victory over lust the way we are expected to win over worry or greed or malice. Rather, Paul instructs Timothy, and thus us, not to conquer or stand and fight, or pray about or resolve, but to *flee* lust."[2]

However, whether one finds a way to escape or not often has to do with the health of his or her marriage in the first place. Most affairs have far deeper roots than a brief temptation, roots that involve serious problems in the marriage itself.

But in a way, that fact is an important source of hope for recovery *after* marital trust has been broken. If infidelity usually springs from problems that can be faced and solved, then a marriage—even when trust has been broken—*can* be put back together.

The true stories in this book are good examples. They involve couples who have experienced broken trust but have found their way back to wholeness and health. It has not been easy for them to recount the pain they've been through. But they are willing to share their stories to give you a glimpse of the same hope that rescued their marriages.

Each couple has participated in Recovery of Hope, a program sponsored by a network of counseling centers around the country. Every day, marital conflicts are resolved, hurts are healed, brokenness is made whole, but most people do not hear about these successes. And because they do not hear the accounts of restored marriages, they have no hope when their own marriage gets in trouble. The Recovery of Hope Network has helped hundreds of couples recover hope in their marriage primarily by giving them an opportunity to hear other couples, who have been through the worst, tell their stories of reconciliation. The message is clear: With help, marriages can be restored.

Throughout the book and especially in the fourth chapter, Dr. Steve Wilke provides insights into why and how trust breaks down in marriages and how trust and intimacy can be rebuilt. Dr. Wilke is a professional counselor and president of Recovery of Hope.

Dave and Neta Jackson
Evanston, Illinois

CHAPTER ONE

Change Her? Change Him?
No, Change Me

Mark poked his head into the hospital room. "Hi, girls! Are you ready?" His blue eyes twinkled, and he was grinning from ear to ear.

Dark-haired Nina managed a smile. It was depressing to put her maternity clothes back on, but none of her regular clothes fit yet. She moved gingerly as she packed her things, trying not to think about the two hundred stitches that were holding her bottom together. It had been an excruciating delivery; the baby had come faster than expected with no time to do an episiotomy. The internal tearing had been like "an implosion," the doctor said.

The nurse was holding baby Erin, all wrapped up in her new outfit from Grandma, ready for her debut into the world. "Come to Daddy, Sweetheart," Mark crooned, taking his newborn in one arm and picking up Nina's suitcase in the other. The nurse maneuvered Nina into a wheelchair, then had to practically trot to keep up with Mark's fast pace down the hall.

What's the hurry? thought Nina, for whom every movement was uncomfortable. But she dismissed the thought; she just wanted to get home.

"Home" was a large house shared with five other young men doing voluntary service work for whom Mark and Nina Samuels served as house parents. The Vietnam War was in full swing, but Mark, age twenty, and the other young men were conscientious objectors doing two years of voluntary service working with kids in a poor area of Tampa.

All the guys gave the new little family a rousing welcome. "Congratulations, you two!" "Ho boy, she's cute." "Here, I'll take the suitcase."

Nina smiled gamely, but was grateful

when they were finally in their bedroom and she could sink down on the bed. She just wanted to stay there all day and be taken care of.

Mark put the baby in the waiting bassinet, brought a couple more pillows for Nina, then said cheerfully, "Well, are you OK now? All settled? The guys are waiting—we're a little late."

Nina looked confused. "What do you mean, late? Where are you going?"

"Honey, you know. Today's the day we're taking the neighborhood kids waterskiing. It's been scheduled for weeks."

"But . . ." Nina squeezed her eyes shut to blink back the tears, "but that's before we knew the baby would be coming home today."

"Exactly!" Mark said patiently, scratching his reddish beard. "If we had known the baby was going to come two weeks early, we'd have picked a different day. But," he added as he bent and wiggled Erin's toes, "babies don't announce these things."

"But I don't want you to go," Nina whispered.

"Hey. I can't disappoint the kids. I'll be back tonight. Erin's not going to miss her daddy for just one day. We've got lots of time to get acquainted." Mark grabbed his jacket, then turned back. "Now, Honey, you just rest. I'll be back tonight. Bye!"

In a few minutes Nina heard the van pull out of the driveway. The house was silent. Then, rolling over onto her side, she let the tears come, hot and furious. *I hate him!* her mind screamed. *Just once I wish he'd think of me instead of himself!*

The gang of six came home loud and happy after a day on the water. Mark came in the bedroom moaning in mock agony. He took off his shirt, revealing a sunburn, and lay face down on the bed. "Hey, Honey," he said, his voice muffled in the covers, "can you find something to put on my back? It's killing me."

With difficulty, Nina got up, found the burn medicine in the bathroom, and mechanically rubbed it on his back. As he told her about all the fun they'd had that day, he didn't seem to notice that she didn't say a thing.

Raised in a religious family, Mark Samuels brought to his marriage a traditional understanding of husband-wife roles and expectations. He understood his role as providing for his family, being honest at work, being responsible for his commitments, and staying loyal to his beliefs as a Christian. As head of the household, he would make the final decisions when he and his wife didn't agree.

His understanding of Nina's role was also traditional. She would stay home and raise their children. He would provide for their needs financially, and she would take care of the housework and child care.

Nina, on the other hand, had her own expectations for a husband. "I wanted a strong man who would cherish me, treat me lovingly, and never, never ignore me. I wanted a husband who would understand me and respect my opinions."

Within the first six months of marriage, Mark and Nina began to have problems. It started with a call from his draft board. As a member of a "peace church" denomination, Mark was able to file as a conscientious objector. "But," he told Nina, "I'm not trying to get off easy. Some of my friends are going to Vietnam. If I'm going to do alternative service, it should be sacrificial, too."

Mark decided to do his two years with Mennonite Voluntary Service (VS). He and Nina attended an orientation meeting, then talked with another married couple who had done alternative service. It would mean a move, sharing a house with other "VSers," working for almost nothing (each adult got ten dollars a month spending money), and coming home after two years flat broke. The other couple tried to be honest about the challenges. "It basically means sacrificing your marriage for a few years," they said.

"Mark, please don't do this!" Nina begged tearfully.

But Mark's mind was set; this was important to him. "I knew Nina didn't want to go," he says. "She wanted me to accept a job with the government's I-W program, where we would have had a salary and maybe wouldn't have had to move. But I assumed she would learn, as all wives do, to be happy and content in whatever her husband has chosen for them."

A few months after they arrived at their assignment in Tampa, the Samuels learned they were expecting their first child. Again, Nina begged Mark to leave the program and return home where they could have the baby surrounded by relatives and friends, with the necessary income to start a family, but her wishes were in vain. Nina decided finishing voluntary service was more important to Mark than she was.

"Nina hated voluntary service," Mark admits. "She resented the time I spent waterskiing with the neighborhood kid's ski club and wanted me to spend all my free time with her and the baby. I thought it was just voluntary service and being far away from home that she didn't like. But even after we returned home to Pennsylvania, she seemed to complain more and more."

"And the two will become one." The question is . . . which one did they become?

Every couple defines the way their mar-

riage will work. Mark and Nina assumed their own ideas of a marriage were standard marital fare. What seemed obvious to her seemed like excessive demands to him; choices made by him were experienced by her as incredible insensitivity. The result was ever increasing bitterness, rage, and frustration. What husband could be so cruel? Did all wives complain so much? Why was this happening? They loved each other.

Mark loved Nina the way he thought a husband should. Nina loved Mark. Few things in life are as painful as misunderstood love. With the Samuels, the situation looked like the conflict. What Mark and Nina didn't realize was that changing the situation didn't change who they were as persons, or how they related.

Marriage deserves a custom fit. The tailoring process requires both the man and the woman to be flexible—open—together.

Back in Pennsylvania, a baby boy joined the family, keeping Nina busy at home. Mark plunged into life with his usual gusto, working hard at his job but also finding time for fishing and hunting and playing on a local softball team.

To Nina, her entire life seemed determined by Mark's wants and needs. They would rush through dinner—leaving the dishes on the table—to get to his ball games on time. "Never mind that I would have to do the dishes several hours later after keeping up with two bored preschoolers," she remembers.

Not that Nina kept quiet about her feelings. "If it's not softball, it's fishing!" she often fumed. "Why don't you spend some time just being at home with me and the kids?"

"I do spend time with the kids. Why do you think I want you and the kids to come to the ball games? So we can be together as a family!"

"You want me to support your activities, but you don't help with things around here."

"For goodness' sake, Nina, I work long hours supporting this family. You're home all day; taking care of the kids and doing the housework is your job."

"Sure, you work eight hours a day,

but at least you get off work! When does my job end?"

Mark sighed patiently. "Your problem is you're a perfectionist. What's a little mess? You've got to change your expectations about housework to fit the realities of a growing family."

"But you never help around the house!"

"That's not true. I just don't think I should have to tell the team that their catcher can't play tonight because he's home doing the dishes—just so our house can win some award for *Good Housekeeping!*"

To pacify Nina's complaints, Mark would sometimes say no to his fishing buddies, help put the kids to bed, and take a turn at dishes. But he felt henpecked. Couldn't a man enjoy a little fishing or hunting? Was he supposed to run a vacuum cleaner or change diapers with all his free time? He was a good husband, after all. He had a good job, he was faithful, and he didn't get angry or lose control easily—in spite of all her complaining. In return, a wife was supposed to support her husband's interests, not nag him to death.

As the kids grew and needed more space, the Samuels moved to a huge house in the country in exchange for caring for the livestock, plus lawn and property upkeep. They also decided to accept care for a troubled teenager who needed a foster home.

Meanwhile, Mark had changed jobs to a commission-only sales job. So now, in addition to two children, a troubled teenage girl, and some of the farm work, Nina took a job waitressing. "It was not at all unusual for me to sleep only three to four hours a day," she says.

One night their foster daughter struck out at Nina, bending her glasses and swelling her nose. Nina appealed to Mark for help. But he did not rush to her defense as she thought he would. "You pushed her too hard, Nina," he said. "Ease up a little. You should try to understand her more. Then she won't lash out at you."

Nina was stunned. Already exhausted and feeling unloved, her sense of personhood withered even more. She felt worthless, little more to Mark than a maid and a sex object. Recalling that event, Nina says, "I vacillated between being furious and wanting out of this painful relationship to being utterly sad that our marriage was not working. The pain was like an open wound in the center of my being. I felt like I was being destroyed piece by piece."

Like a dog chasing its tail, the futility continued. The lingering life issues were never addressed.

Pleas for Mark to stay at home felt to him like being nagged to death. He missed Nina's cry for attention.

Mark's running the show was experienced as domination. She missed seeing his love for her—shown the best he knew how. Their love was battered day after day after day.

Mark and Nina continued in a state of conflict for eleven years. The more she complained and begged, the more defensive he became. Typical arguments went something like this . . .

"You never listen to me! My opinions never count with you. You always find a way to do what you want to do, but never what I want to do!"

"Always? Never? The truth is, Nina, you have never learned to submit to doing anything my way. As the head of this house, God has given me authority to make decisions I think are best for this family."

"Best for the family? All you care about is yourself. You don't love me. I don't think you ever did!"

"Look, Nina, every couple has their disagreements. Just because we don't see eye to eye about everything doesn't mean I don't love you."

"Oh, really? If you loved me, you'd care about what I think. You'd listen to my suggestions; you'd do what I want to do once in a while!"

"Wasn't the trip to Nashville your idea?"

"Oh sure. But that's just because it didn't conflict with anything you wanted to do. When we disagree about something, you never follow my suggestion."

"That's just the point! Someone has to make the decision when we don't agree. That's the role of the husband. You may not like it, but that's what the Bible says: 'Wives, submit yourselves to your husband.'"

"Well, I don't like it! I don't think the Bible means you're supposed to ignore me. You never spend time with me. I've had it! I don't have to stay in this marriage."

Mark assumed that these kinds of misunderstandings and personality conflicts were a normal part of married life—until Nina started threatening to move out. "So," he says, "I tried to pacify her complaints. I quit fishing, stopped playing softball, didn't go hunting. But nothing seemed to make much difference. The bitterness and distance between us just seemed to be getting worse and worse."

"It's already over; why keep pretending?" Nina said.

"You can't move out. We agreed for better or worse, remember? Separation isn't an option."

"Oh, yeah? Watch me!"

Mark began to panic. What would people say? What would happen to the kids? What would God think? If Nina divorced him, he couldn't even be an active church member anymore. He determined to find some way to make her change her mind.

Respect, affirmation, appreciation—both Mark and Nina sought emotional nourishment from each other, but they stayed just out of reach. As the desperation grew, a demanding spirit took over. "Be the way I tell you to be!" underscored each fight.

Always relegated to the back seat, Nina lived in fear. What did she fear? Nothing less than the loss of her own personhood.

Primarily in control of the marriage, Mark feared Nina's input. What did he fear? He thought her input meant his failure as a husband. Just as Nina's personhood was linked to collaboration and equal partnership, for Mark her input was a threat to his identity as the successful family leader doing things the right way for everyone.

They were so set in their ways and drowning in so much pain that mandates for the other went unaccepted. The light of hope was dimmed by despair.

As things came to a crisis, Nina kept wondering, "How can two people who once loved each other and who share two beautiful children experience so much hurt? Why can't Mark understand my needs for respect and appreciation?"

Nina failed to see why she should submit to her husband. What in the world did being submissive mean, anyway? "Once when we were cleaning the barn between flocks of chickens," she recalls. "A second story floor board where I was standing broke. I was shaken, nervous, and bleeding where the broken board scraped my leg. Mark wanted me to bandage my leg and hurry back to finish the job. Was that being submissive? It certainly didn't feel good, didn't feel like being loved."

The long painful discussions, all her tears, and even shouting were to no avail. "More and more my ultimatum about separation seemed like the only option," Nina recalls. "I could not go on with this constant friction." She knew Mark wouldn't leave, and she also didn't want to disrupt the children's lives any more than necessary. If she was going to leave Mark, she'd have to leave alone.

As time passed, it became clear that Nina was serious about leaving. "Changing Nina's mind was clearly not working," Mark says. "For the first time, I began to frantically look at myself as well as at Nina to see what was wrong." Help came in the form of one of his coworkers who was in the process of divorcing her husband. Mark worked up the courage to talk to Marcie about what was happening with them; she seemed to be able to relate to almost every problem he and Nina had.

"In talking with Marcie, I identified— without all the emotional interference— a number of major issues that were strictly mine," Mark remembers. "She helped me see that my desire for control and authority was more an indication of my selfishness than it was a desire to follow Christ. She also gave me some marriage books to read that pointed a finger more at me than at Nina. I was shocked! I thought I had to change Nina, but I was beginning to see that I needed to change myself. Nina was right; I didn't really know how to love her. I had always assumed that if I fulfilled my responsibilities, that was love."

Mark's world turned upside down. He was discovering that love is more than fulfilling one's obligations. For the first time, he realized he'd used being "head of the house" as an excuse to get his own way— and to ignore Nina's pain. Somehow he had missed a critical ingredient in what it meant to be a leader in his family. Control, authority, making final decisions . . . these definitions ignored the needs of the very person he loved most.

What a struggle those new ideas were! But, armed with these new insights, Mark thought if he could get Nina to believe he was willing to change, she wouldn't go through with the separation. He pleaded and bargained and tried to implement some changes as quickly as he could—asking her input about decisions, taking more initiative to do housework and child care, doing things he knew she wanted to do. It didn't work. She thought he was only pretending in order to get her to stay.

"Convinced I needed to change anyway," he says, "I began an all-out effort. Being able to bounce things off Marcie at work was very helpful. Although Nina never really appreciated the struggles I was going through or the extent that I was changing, I was almost proud of myself."

Nina made arrangements to rent the third floor of a house from a woman with whom she worked. "Little did I realize what separation would ultimately mean," she says now. "Initially there was a great deal of relief to be away from all the arguments and from trying to live up to Mark's expectation of what a wife should be—in spite of hurtful things said by well-meaning friends and the loneliness of going home to an empty room."

Nina had announced in early summer that she was leaving when school started, so by September Mark was pretty well adjusted to the idea that she was leaving. He thought he was prepared to keep house and raise Erin and Christopher, now nine and six. But the reality of Nina actually moving out—

enduring the long evenings, putting the children to bed, cooking, helping with school work, doing laundry, and sleeping alone—was far worse than he had imagined.

"I discovered how little I really knew about taking care of my children," Mark admits. "But I was determined not to give up. I was going to prove to Nina that, instead of not being able to make it by myself like she thought, I was going to be a super single father. Armed with that kind of arrogant pride and self-determination, I accepted—for now—that my wife had left me."

When a couple is stalemated, one partner may feel driven to do something—anything!—to reduce the friction and change the situation. Changing the situation, while providing some relief, rarely solves the problems and often presents new ones as well.

The opportunity for real change had always been there. But with an uncharted future and their present in turmoil, change was no longer an option—it was a necessity. Along with the opportunity to change, however, came the questions and strong emotions: "What have I done? Who should I blame? What should I do?"

Nina soon discovered that parenting from two separate households brought a whole new set of problems without solving any of their basic ongoing ones. Suddenly she became the outsider, even though she continued to see the children every day and be involved in their care.

"I went to all the trouble to leave him and still felt like Mark didn't take me seriously!" Nina says. "He seemed to think that once I saw what a great dad and housekeeper he was, I'd come running back. Even though we separated to gain some space and new perspective, I filed for divorce to prove I meant what I said. As long as his changes were only to get me back, I needed to get further away emotionally."

When Mark decided to contest the divorce, Nina spent hours crying till there were no tears left to cry. She drew up a bill of particulars—writing down everything she could remember in eleven years of marriage that would convince a judge that she should be allowed to be divorced from Mark.

Divorce. "I was finding that word a misnomer," Nina admits. "Unless one parent is willing to walk away from the children, you never really get away from your spouse. We had to continue to relate on some level."

Custody was a difficult issue. If Mark and Nina couldn't agree on the arrangements for the children, they would be taken into court and asked with which parent they wanted to live. "What a devastating thing to do to a child! Would there be no end to the pain from the terrible mistake we made when we married?" Nina wondered desperately.

In spite of the fact that Nina had not only left, but also filed for divorce, Mark did not give in to despair. He clung to a seed of hope that had been sown when he first began to see his own need to change. Hope is cultivated as we allow God's work to transform us.

During their discussions Mark's co-worker had admitted that she really didn't want a divorce, but she was convinced her husband would never change. Her admission gave Mark hope. "If *I* continue to change, maybe Nina will notice and reconsider."

He continued to read and study, mostly from the Scriptures. The apostle Paul's teaching that husbands should love their wives "as Christ loved the church" was a revelation. Christ loved His bride sacrificially, laying down His own life. This insight into what it really meant to be "head of his family" also gave Mark hope. "If I can learn even a little of that kind of love, maybe Nina will change her mind," he thought.

That Scripture also helped Mark deal with Nina's rejection. "God does not stop loving me just because I stop loving Him. If I'm supposed to love like God does, I need to learn to love regardless of how my love is received."

Although idealistic, Mark says this was how he disciplined himself to learn how to love, respect, and care. He knew there were no guarantees—only hope. But he committed himself to hoping and loving as long as Nina was still his legal wife.

In the meantime, life had to go on. Mark bought a small house in a nearby town and moved off the farm. Helping the children adjust to a new school and neighborhood, fixing up the house, and working fifty hours a week kept him busy. He also played guitar and sang in a contemporary Christian band.

"That helped me survive," he says. "We rehearsed every Tuesday evening and often talked for long hours afterwards. That kind of support, along with the fun and spirit-building concerts, challenged me as a person and helped me keep my goal of learning to love Nina in focus."

Keeping hope alive over a long period of time, however, was the biggest struggle. "I was so lonely. Many well-meaning church friends counseled me to accept reality and move on with my life. Others just didn't know what to say or how to act around a guy who's separated. Only once during the three years we were separated did anyone sit with me in church. I either sat with someone already seated or I sat alone."

Repeated rejection from Nina also

kept chipping away at Mark's foundation of hope. One Sunday he called to invite her to go along with him and the kids to the museum. A man answered the phone; when Nina finally came to the phone she was laughing and having a great time. "Go to the museum with you? No, I don't think so." The foundation of hope nearly crumbled.

Temptation to quit also came from another coworker who "fell in love" with Mark and tried her best to get him to "love" her. Sarah called him at home, came to talk cozily after the kids were in bed, and was always warm and friendly at work.

"Sarah," he explained patiently, "I'm still married. As long as we're not divorced, I have hope that Nina and I will get back together."

"Yes, but you need to be loved, too," she kept saying.

But, Mark says, "I had made so many mistakes before that I was determined not to add unfaithfulness to the list."

The hope that he nurtured didn't take away the long, lonely evenings or the always present pain of failure, but it did provide strength, purpose, and a sense of integrity that helped prepare Mark for the difficult process of putting his relationship with Nina back together.

During marital stress, feelings cry out for relief. As with a broken leg, the pain is real. Medication only deadens the pain; healing makes the bone strong again. With emotional pain, it's tempting to beg for something—anything!—to kill the pain.

Each person tolerates pain differently. Mark had found a glimmer of hope, supported by perseverance, principles, and prayer to keep the healing process on course. Nina, on the other hand, had felt discounted and unloved for years. Her trust in Mark had eroded long ago; she didn't really believe he was capable of change. When she left him, she was especially vulnerable to someone else who showed care and compassion.

For Nina, hope was more elusive and was preceded by despair of life itself. The Samuels had been separated a year when Mark and the children moved into town. This meant that Nina could no longer see the children every day. At about the same time, she ended an intimate relationship with another man which had begun early in their separation and lasted more than a year.

"The loss of this close relationship left a terrible void in my life," Nina says. "My friends applauded my decision, assured me I was better off without him, and promptly changed the subject. No one shared my grieving process. How could I survive these two simultaneous losses? In spite of all else, I had continued to be a good mother. Seeing so much less of Erin and Christopher cut into my last bit of self-esteem."

One night Nina decided the pain was unbearable. She wrote long notes to the children, swallowed several handfuls of prescription medicines, washed them down with half a bottle of alcohol, and lay down to die. Shortly afterwards the phone rang. The friend on the other end—a nurse—realized Nina needed urgent help. She alerted Nina's pastor and wife and the three of them came to her apartment. They dragged her out of bed, carried her around, poured caffeine into her, and checked her vital signs for several hours before taking her to the pastor's house for the night.

Nina came so close to taking her life. And yet, the end of the road can be a turning point rather than a dead end. Up until now Nina and Mark had been coping with their separation on their own. "Advice," some helpful and some not, came from well-meaning friends and relatives. Interestingly, however, even though their marriage was in crisis, they had never seen a counselor. That was about to change.

After a few days Nina went back to her apartment, but it was the beginning of the long, often difficult but steady road back to health . . . and Mark.

Nina speaks with gratefulness about her pastor and his wife, from whom she received much counsel and who, in a lot of ways, became surrogate parents, especially the pastor whom she now calls "Dad."

"Their warm parenting, wise guidance, willingness to give many hours—often at inconvenient times—and unwavering caring enabled me to re-

cover a sense of personhood," she says.
"I had made some terrible mistakes,
wrong and costly choices, but Dad especially helped me realize I could be forgiven. I could start again. I was not
worthless."

The fact that her pastor and his wife,
who knew the worst about her, did not
reject, berate, or give up on her, helped
Nina experience something of God's un-
conditional love. "I began to realize my
failure in marriage was not total failure," she says. "Their love and acceptance of me was not dependent on my
willingness to reconcile to Mark. Once I
accused them of caring solely because
they wanted to get Mark and me back
together. 'Nina,' Dad said, 'we've never
even prayed for that.' Eventually I knew
that I was valued just because I am me."

There were lots of tears and struggles
as Nina grew from emotional infancy.
Her feelings vacillated from childlike
adoration of her pastor and his wife to
rebellion and anger as she sorted
through her beliefs and understandings.
But along the way she had a growing

conviction that God, too, accepted and loved her.

With a recovering sense of personhood, Nina was able to reevaluate the relationships in her life. Was it possible to consider withdrawing the divorce proceedings? Mark had been changing a lot—taking responsibility for the kids, doing housework, reaching out to her. She had assumed it was just a ruse to get her back, that he'd go back to his old ways once she was back in the home. But . . . was it possible he really was changing? Could she and Mark each be whole enough individually that they could put their relationship back together?

Through sheer determination Mark decided he had to change. He would make healthy changes whether Nina came back to him or not. The tug-of-war was over; Mark had dropped the rope. Nina responded. She desired to be a healthy person also.

Only when individuals give up trying to change their spouses and concentrate on

*changing themselves can a marriage be-
gin to be built again.*

Nina's pastor was delighted but cautious
when their counseling sessions began to
include conversation about a possible
reconciliation. He didn't try to make it
seem easy. Mark and Nina had been
separated more than two years and
there was a lot to consider.

"Nina," he said, "forgiveness is
needed on both sides. Before you will be
ready to resume intimacy with Mark,
emotionally or physically, you will need
to forgive him for all the times you have
felt ignored and discounted, for all the
times he has treated you badly, for the
difficult voluntary service experiences.
You will both need to choose to respect
and care for the feelings of the other."

As for Mark, he was excited that Nina
wanted to talk about reconciliation. The
early conversations were through the
pastor or by phone. "But I was beginning to see some light at the end of what
had seemed like a dark, unending tun-
nel. For two and a half years I had fan-
tasized about this moment and how

different I was going to be. Now here it was, about to happen!"

Some of the changes Mark had vowed to make were about to be tested. "Early in our separation," he remembers, "I had promised myself that I was going to keep a short list of hurts. If I was really serious about waiting for Nina, I was going to have to forgive her as I went along for the hurts, loneliness, and pain of the separation—or when the time came, I would be the one who would be unwilling to accept her back. And so I did. And I thought I had done a pretty good job, too. So I was eager to be reconciled."

A time was set for Nina to come to the house so they could talk about what needed to happen. After the kids were in bed, they went to the kitchen to talk. Mark was not prepared for what happened next.

Nina began by confessing her year-long affair. She tried to convey that she was sorry, that she felt badly it had happened. "But," she said finally, trying to be honest, "I still have warm feelings for him. If you can't deal with that, we might as well not talk about reconciliation any further."

Mark was stunned. Suddenly, lots of loose ends seemed to fit together. All the little hints he'd been getting from friends at church . . . the times a man had answered her phone . . . Nina filing for a divorce . . . maybe even her moving out in the first place. "I've waited this long," he heard himself mumbling, "I'm not going to quit now." But he was crushed.

When Nina left that night, Mark plunged into an emotional tailspin. How could he have been so naive! He felt betrayed. Had she lied to him? Did she really want the separation to gain space—or did she already have a boyfriend? "I don't remember much else about that first conversation," Mark says, "except that she also hated my house, said she wouldn't live there, and that if we were going to get back together we'd have to move."

Thus began the worst week for Mark of their entire separation. All the past hurts that he thought he'd forgiven came back with a vengeance. He began to wonder if reconciliation was such a good idea after all. "But," he says, "it led to one of the most sacred experiences of my life. By the end of that week my anger had subsided enough that I knelt beside my bed and asked God to help me, once again, to forgive Nina. Immediately a voice in my head said, 'You can't forgive her; look what she's done to you!'"

For the next hour, all the buried hurts that he had filed against Nina were brought up one by one. As he faced each one Mark said, "Lord, I forgive Nina for . . ." and named the specific hurt. To each the voice would reply, "Yes, but . . ." and on it went. Three or four times Mark remembers agreeing that "I can't forgive her for that." And each time another Voice seemed to say, "But I forgave you."

After a long pause Mark replied, "OK, Lord, I forgive Nina for that, too."

"Finally," Mark says, "the first voice was quiet, and I went to bed. I woke up a changed person. Once again I was excited about reconciliation."

"Don't let her off the hook. Her sin is greater than mine!"

But if we don't forgive, we are hurt again every time we dwell on what someone else has done. Forgiveness is in many ways doing ourselves a favor, says Louis B. Smedes in his book, *Forgive and Forget.* Forgiveness gives us the freedom to begin a new relationship with the person we've forgiven.

Knowing that sin hurts both the sinner and the sinned against, Jesus spoke to the woman accused of adultery: *"Neither do I condemn you; go and sin no more."* The goal of forgiveness is healing.

For about six months before she actually moved in, Nina and Mark went through a process of carefully constructed compromises. "We made lists of areas that needed to be negotiated," Nina says. "We talked about our expectations, frequently including the children. I was the outsider moving into their space. For instance, my standards of housekeeping were different from theirs; we compromised by allowing the bedrooms to be kept to their liking but agreeing to keep the living areas according to my definition of 'neat.' We also agreed to remodel the present house, with a firm commitment to move within three years."

Both Mark and Nina curtailed church and community involvements to focus on family healing and rebuilding. In those six months they attempted to address everything they could think of to build trust and mutual understanding. For instance, even though they had negotiated a lot of practical issues, Nina wondered, "In what ways have each of us changed that will enable us to have a better marriage? We argue about the dirty car or who will carry out the garbage, but those are only symptoms of deeper problems. Until we address the real issues, there will be a never-ending supply of surface aggravations."

To help them examine those issues, they scheduled several sessions with a family counselor. There they began to see that the difficulty was not primarily in the marriage, but within themselves—especially in unresolved problems from their families of origin.

Nina began to realize she was rebelling against the relationship her parents had. "My mother seemed like a non-person. She had no opinions about anything unless she first checked with my father. This made me determined to voice my opinions regardless of what my husband thought, making it extremely difficult for me to accept Mark's ideas and decisions and leading, unfortunately, to a lot of unnecessary disagreements."

Mark adds, "My dad basically ignored my mother when she got upset, so I thought that's just how a man was supposed to respond. The interactions I witnessed taught me not to worry about tears or words spoken emotionally." Based on their past experiences, both Mark and Nina had built walls around themselves, shutting the other out.

During one session, as they argued about an event from years past, the counselor gave them a particularly helpful bit of advice: "You each remember the incident differently, and neither of you will significantly change your recollections, so there's nothing to be

gained by arguing. Reality falls somewhere between your two differing per-
ceptions, and neither is right or wrong."

*As most couples do, Mark and Nina both
had to learn to listen to, accept, and respect each other. They discovered their
own experiences and feelings might be
different, even in the same situation.
When each felt heard by the other, they
could then work out common solutions,
taking the other's experiences and feelings
into account.*

Mark had been publicly humiliated
when the divorce papers had been
served at his place of work and a notice
published in the newspapers, so he and
Nina decided to hold a public service
celebrating their reconciliation. They
greeted families and friends at the
church for music and sharing in recognition of their journey and intention to
live together again. Three years and two
months after their separation, Nina
moved back.

"But having Nina move in with me
again was just the first step," Mark admits, "the beginning of what was to

become a lifelong process of learning to really know and love the beautiful women that I married. And," he admits, "learning to know myself."

Sitting beside dark-haired Nina, his blue eyes sparkling above his reddish beard, Mark states the obvious. "We are two completely different people! In spite of all my philosophical changes and new spiritual insights into how a husband should love his wife, I am still the same person. Even learning how I became the way I am, even knowing who and what I want to become, hasn't erased all traces of the old habit patterns. I'm finding that I need to continually work on becoming the husband God wants me to be."

Even though they have been together again for over eight years, Mark and Nina recently went for counseling to help iron out a communication problem. "We've come a long way," explains Nina, "but sometimes we still miscommunicate. I guess it can be boiled down to how we use words! When I first went to kindergarten, I was very shy and spoke softly. My teacher misunderstood my name and wrote down *Nita*. My mother thought I had lied about my name! Right then and there I decided I would always be very precise about my words and what I meant. So I choose words to say exactly what I mean." She glances at her husband. "Mark, on the other hand, puts much more weight on body language and tone of voice. He's always telling me what I mean in spite of what my words say! Then sometimes I repeat back his exact words to him, and he says, 'But that's not what I meant!'"

So now they are learning to accept their different approaches to communication. "I agreed to listen to the *meanings* behind Mark's words," she says. "And Mark is learning to accept my words at face value, instead of him telling *me* what I mean!"

Accepting and respecting differences rather than trying to change the other spouse is a fundamental marital challenge. Seeing the "splinter" in the other's eye is easy; seeing the "logs" in our own is, oh, so hard. It takes God-given grace to deal first with our own imperfections.

This grace hasn't come easy for Mark and Nina. But if asked, both would say the effort and the gift are worth it.

Mark sums up some of the things he and Nina have learned. "We have more realistic expectations of marriage and each other. We respect each person's uniqueness. Housework is shared—"

Nina cuts in. "Well, at least we're working on that one! But I now know it's important to share 'people time' even though the floor is dusty and the laundry is not all finished. I am more comfortable with who I am and no longer feel personally insulted when Mark disagrees with me."

Both Mark and Nina admit it is difficult to balance work, family, church, community, and personal involvements, and this occasionally leads to intense discussions. "But," Mark hastens to add, "they are no longer primarily personal attacks or attempts to change the other person. We know our relationship is important and valuable."

Nina smiles. "Sometimes I'm surprised at how much we enjoy being together, taking walks, playing Scrabble, laughing at silly jokes and sometimes even at ourselves." Taking Mark's hand she adds, "The past is behind us. I'm glad we're together again and still working at loving each other."

CHAPTER TWO

Seeds of Destruction, Seeds of Hope

Karen Abbott waited in the living room while Carl answered the hall phone. They were going out. She wasn't sure whether she really wanted to or not—things had been so strained lately. But maybe dinner and a movie would take her mind off their son's belligerent behavior . . . and the deep lurking feeling that something was desperately wrong.

Then she heard Carl lower his voice, but his words seemed to leap with startling clarity into the living room.

"I told you never to call me at home. What is it? . . . No, not now, I really can't . . . OK, OK. I'll call you later."

Karen heard the door to the hall

closet open, and in a moment Carl was by her side with her coat. As she slipped her arm into the sleeve, their eyes met and locked.

The mask on Carl's face that had been keeping her at such a distance suddenly dropped. "Karen," he blurted, "I love her."

His words seemed to hit her in the chest and nearly paralyzed her; then she looked down. "I know," she whispered.

The Abbott's lovely midwestern home seemed to boast the success of their almost twenty-year marriage. Even Carl and Karen had always considered themselves a perfect couple. Sweethearts since they were sixteen years old, they went to high school and college together, married, and produced three beautiful children. Carl, slim and medium height, was a successful lawyer; Karen, petite and auburn-haired, was a full-time mom and active in their church and community as a lay leader and volunteer. Together they threw themselves into business, school, church, Scouts, sports, and all the things a happy middle-class couple raising a family does.

But just before their twentieth wedding anniversary, Carl blurted out those fateful words—"I love her"—and the bottom dropped out of their perfect marriage.

In the beginning Carl's relationship with the other woman had been legitimate—another attorney with whom he was working on a difficult case. The case required Carl to spend a great deal of time with her; it was emotionally involving, and they expended much energy and effort toward preparing their brief.

Meanwhile Karen thought of herself as an "understanding wife and a good Christian" for being so supportive of Carl's professional demands and so capable of managing the home front. For several months she was both father and mother to the two children still at home as Carl spent longer and longer hours on the job.

Exactly when Karen's trust and understanding gave way to resentment, then fear, is hard to pinpoint. Maybe it was the morning Carl pulled on the clean socks and shirt she had just put in the drawer the day before and left with nothing more than a hurried "Bye." Or maybe it was the phone calls that seemed more and more frequent: "Karen? It's Carl. I'm going to be late again. Tell the kids I'm sorry. Can you hang in there for me tonight?"

Even when he was lying beside her in the bed they had shared for almost two decades, Carl seemed very far away. Unwilling to crack the veneer on their storybook marriage, Karen said nothing. But the bedroom clock ticking past two . . . two-thirty . . . then three o'clock in the morning found her lying awake staring into the darkness. Finally, grabbing a robe, she would go sit in the bathroom with the door closed so no one would hear her. Then the tears quickly became wracking sobs: "He doesn't love me anymore!"

When the trembling and crying finally stopped, Karen would go back to bed, fall asleep, get up at seven o'clock, and go on with "life as usual" because she didn't know what else to do.

When Carl confessed the affair, Karen felt betrayed—betrayed by the person she trusted the most. "How can this be happening to me? Me!" her mind screamed. "I've worked so hard at doing all the right things. I'm honest, I make a pleasant home, I'm a good cook, I care for the children, I love my husband and children, I've never even been tempted to look at another man outside my marriage. Why, why, why is this happening to me?" She felt as if someone had suddenly hit her in the back with an axe. Hurt, disbelief, fear, loneliness, and anger—the pain was excruciating.

Does a "perfect" marriage suddenly break up on the rocks of infidelity for no reason? No. Acts of infidelity follow from individual and marital problems.

No act of infidelity is ever justified. Infidelity still involves decisions in which one is held personally responsible. However, the quality and nature of a marital relationship does provide the context in which faithfulness is maintained or lost. We come to marriage imperfect, needy, and hurt. Carl and Karen had a marriage which seemed "perfect." But long before the affair, unspoken choices were made that led to what seemed to be the sudden breakup of a perfect marriage.

Every marriage has seeds for growth and seeds for destruction. All marriages have problems. As we continue to learn more about Carl and Karen, watch for the seeds that produced destruction prior to the affair, and watch for how these same problems became seeds of personal and marital growth.

Both Carl and Karen grew up in traditional homes where a concept was deeply ingrained: "If there are problems in the family, keep them to yourselves." Even more than that, both had a view of marriage that seemed to preclude problems.

"It was the Cinderella and Prince Charming fairy tale," Karen says now. "You know, the one that ends 'and they lived happily ever after.' I really believed that if I was a good wife and mother and community volunteer that we would have no problems. Oh sure, we'd have the usual ones—broken arms or illness, and we'd have to scrape by financially in the early years. But those problems didn't faze me. I could be calm in a crisis; I was a good money manager and careful shopper. Certainly, there would never be any real problems with my *marriage*."

With the soberness that comes from having stared reality in the face, Karen adds, "My unreality about life was itself a problem. Since I had grown up thinking that 'good' marriages didn't have problems, I hid even from myself the things that bothered me in my relationship with Carl."

Carl also married to live "happily ever after." But Carl, more than Karen, realized it wasn't working. "I tried hard," he says, "tried to be a good husband and father, tried to be close to Karen. But things seemed to be falling apart. For several years our teenage son had been abusing alcohol and other drugs; the situation was beginning to feel unbearable. I felt hopeless and helpless; I wasn't in control."

A second event also jarred Carl to the

core. One night the phone rang. It was Carl's father: "It's your brother Nick. There's been an accident—Nick's dead." Carl was stunned. His younger brother was an exceptionally caring person that Carl looked to a lot as a model. Why Nick of all people? Nothing was making sense.

When Carl woke up the next morning, and the next and the next, the depression that settled on him didn't go away. Even his career, which in the early years had been stimulating and rewarding, had lost its meaning. After twenty years of marriage it seemed that nothing from the past counted. Carl looked at his wife and realized she seemed like a stranger.

Then came the affair with another woman, driving Carl to the depths of overwhelming guilt and shame. In the short span of three months, the Abbott's "perfect marriage," done "by the book" right out of the 1950s, exploded in their faces. Carl felt as if he had crashed headlong into a wall.

Later Carl was able to identify that wall as a pretty classic "male mid-life crisis."

Locked in a belief that emotional problems, hurts, and desires were not to be discussed or even acknowledged stopped the chance for changes and adaptations along the way to occur. After a couple of decades, the kettle blew. Like anything left unattended, when recognition came, a major crisis occurred. Now the option for minor changes along the way was no longer adequate. At the point of crisis, only significant changes suffice.

Unable to acknowledge their own personal issues, Carl and Karen had never experienced true open and honest sharing. Neither partner knew how to deal with their own internal issues, much less those of their spouse. They had yet to discover that all of us are created as emotional and spiritual beings, and it's essential that we be in tune with our emotions and God's desires for our life.

Carl confessed his involvement with the other woman out of desperation. He had to stop this crazy tailspin. But as he sat with his wife, telling her to her face that there was another woman, he felt terrified that he would lose Karen, too.

Somewhere, down under it all, she was still the most important person in the world to him. But he felt confused because some of the time he didn't feel he loved her at all—or even cared.

"Karen," he pleaded, "I know I don't deserve this. What I did was wrong, and you have a right to be angry. But you need to forgive me. We can't let this destroy us. We have too much at stake."

Karen looked at Carl silently, then looked away. She was angrier than she'd ever been in her life. She finally controlled her voice enough to say, "I can't do that right now. I don't know what I will decide about our marriage. How can I ever trust you again?"

Her anger about the affair translated into one thing for Carl: rejection. He felt like a child, abandoned by his mother in a busy shopping center. Her words, "How can I ever trust you again?" sat like an iron ball in his stomach, and he sank deeper into depression as surely as if he'd fallen into a well. Could he ever be rid of the guilt and shame? Was he an evil, shifty-eyed monster no one could trust?

Putting words on it later, Carl said, "I felt helpless, as though I were hanging, terrified, on the end of a thread over a cliff a thousand feet down while Karen, at the top, held the other end of the thread in one hand and a pair of scissors in the other, trying to decide whether to cut me loose and drop me to the bottom."

Carl prayed a lot—frantic "rescue pleas"—but got little relief, even though he believed God was there and cared. He had no idea what God could do with this mess, so he began to shut God out.

In her shock and anger and grief, Karen wondered what else she'd been blind to, what other problems she'd been relating to with an unreal view of life. She took another long, hard look at the behavior of their oldest child. Their son had gotten involved with alcohol and drugs during junior high and high school. Carl and Karen knew he used marijuana, took pills, and drank too much on occasion; but they didn't know—or chose not to believe—that he was becoming an alcoholic and drug addict.

Karen now says, "Our son was hard-headed, lazy, dishonest, and careless. He didn't behave as we had taught him as a child. This great discrepancy in what he'd been taught and the way he behaved caused me great pain. When I was growing up I got the message that if a kid is a troublemaker in the family, the parents must have done something wrong. What was this saying about me? About our family? I couldn't deal with it, so I became quite depressed and just blocked it out. I walked around like a zombie—didn't laugh, didn't cry a lot, just went on in a hazy, nondescript world with a dull throb in my head and in my heart. And, although I didn't realize it at the time, my relationship with Carl was affected, too."

The simple view that "bad kids are a result of bad parents" traps parents into either unrelenting guilt or the opposite extreme: total denial. It is better to acknowledge each person's individual will and ability to choose. Being a responsible and caring parent does not guarantee that your chil-

dren will be without problems and never make mistakes.

Knowing this can help to open the lines of communication that bring understanding within a family. The goal of parents and children can then be for each to work to enhance each others' lives in a supportive and caring way. As problems surface in the family, the emotional pain and isolation that often provide the seeds for destructive behavior can be faced and openly dealt with.

Locked in a need to look and act like a good family, Carl and Karen missed the clues in and around them.

Because of the stress and depression surrounding their son's alcohol and drug abuse, another area of the Abbotts' life suffered: sex. Although neither Carl nor Karen would have admitted it, sex had been a longstanding and troublesome issue for them. Karen thought sex was fine—after the dishes were done, the kids were asleep, and they were in bed. But Carl had different ideas.

Even when they were dating and for all their married life, Carl longed for physical affection from Karen. *I'll know she really loves me,* he'd think as they drove in the car or watched a movie or just sat and talked, *if she'll run her fingers through my hair or just gently caress my arm.* But those were things Karen simply didn't do. Over the years, Carl's anger silently simmered, his insecurity and lack of trust grew. Did Karen really love him? Why couldn't she be sexually playful and show him she really loved him?

Carl wanted Karen to respond sexually whenever he felt interested— "which," he admits, "seemed like most of the time." Coming into the kitchen where she was peeling potatoes, Carl would spontaneously get aroused and feel like playing. Slipping up behind her he would "lovingly" slip his hands into her bra and fondle her breasts or begin undressing her. He thought she should be flattered and aroused by this attention. Karen usually tolerated the initial advances, but when things got critical she'd get disgusted.

"Stop it, Carl! Can't you see I'm busy? Really! You act as if the world should stop every time you feel sexy." Feeling rejected, Carl would retreat in anger and sulk.

But he continued to try to manipulate the marriage sexually. For years he bought sexy underwear and provocative see-through slinky things for Karen to wear so she would feel more sexy and be prepared to seduce him. The gifts, however, just disappeared into dresser drawers. Carl didn't say anything, but he was hurt and confused. Maybe she didn't really love him. . . .

On rare occasions Carl pressed the issue. "Why?" he asked. "Why don't you respond when I touch you or feel loving?" Karen couldn't answer; already she felt pushed into sexual activities in times and places where she wasn't comfortable. Now she felt pressured to come up with a reason and ended up crying. Carl then felt guilty for making her cry ("something a good husband wouldn't do to his wife," he thought). So he left her alone for a few months or years about "why." But he continued to hope he'd find the missing link in an otherwise ideal marriage.

"Her desire to please me by being sexually playful—in or out of bed—was part of my dream for a perfect marriage," Carl reflects, "so I assumed someday it would happen. I just needed to be alert for the magic moment to occur, so I looked for ways to push it along at every opportunity." Frustrated, confused, and lonely, he continued to fill her Valentine's Day, Christmas, and birthday "secret wish list" with seductive clothing.

But Karen seemed to resent his out-of-bed advances more and more and to care less and less for any sexual encounter. "Each rejection of my advances felt like a rejection of me," recalls Carl. "Each instance increased my doubt about how 'perfect' our marriage really was and whether she loved me."

This added to Carl's confusion because, from all outward appearances, their marriage continued to look—and therefore, by definition, was—fine. Both Karen and Carl had graduated from college; Carl had a graduate degree and a good professional position; they had three beautiful children, in whom they invested enormous energy and time. But even though things "looked good," Carl felt a gnawing sensation deep inside that something wasn't right.

The rejection Carl experienced made him especially vulnerable when he met a woman who seemed warm and responsive to his attentions. Without planning it, without any intention to plunge his marriage into crisis, he quickly fell into an affair. In many ways, Carl was like a little boy seeking reassurance that he was OK. What Carl didn't bargain for was the guilt and shame of what he was doing to his marriage and family and the terror that he might lose everything that he cared about.

The facade was now shattered. Problems were revealed. While the collapse seemed sudden, an examination of the marriage's foundation showed glaring flaws.

Carl and Karen loved and cared for each other. They were not mismatched or incompatible. However, because they did not share their feelings, their mutual understandings were not maintained.

Without understanding they were never able to deal with each other in ways that went beyond trying to be nice and proper people.

Now the perfect marriage was dead; pretenses were gone. The worst that could happen had happened. Finally Carl and Karen faced the ultimate question: *What now?*

After admitting the affair to Karen, Carl quickly broke off the relationship with the other woman. He told the woman he wanted to work on his marriage, and the only way was to end their relationship completely. Terminating the relationship helped him see just how much he had wronged Karen—and how much he needed her forgiveness.

At Karen's request, he also cut off relationships with some other women with whom he was close friends. Karen was afraid that she couldn't trust him with any other woman and desperately needed this action on his part. Was he willing to make changes for her and for their marriage? At first, Carl felt Karen's sweeping demands were unreasonable, paranoid. He saw no reason why he had to go that far. But he finally granted her request, and in doing so, Carl took a small but important step toward rebuilding the trust that had been broken. *Almost unnoticed, a seed of hope was sown.*

Not long after the "explosion," when everything in the marriage seemed splattered, Karen and Carl sat at the kitchen table and had a long discussion.

"I don't want to be single," Carl said, toying with his coffee cup. "I want to be married."

Karen nodded. "Me, too . . . but I'm no longer sure I want to be married to you."

Carl flinched; but frankly, he felt the same way. Did he want to be married to Karen?

"We've invested twenty years in this marriage," he said soberly. "We've got three kids. We've had a lot of good times, too. I'm not sure I want to start over."

They sat silently, each thinking back over the years that had led to this point.

"Twenty years is a lot to lose. Maybe

trying to salvage what we've got is a lot better than starting over."

Karen nodded. "I don't want a divorce until we've at least tried. But . . . it can't be the same. We have to find a new footing to build on."

Carl and Karen also agreed they did not want to fall into a common post-crisis trap. Several of their friends had divorced and remarried, only to find they had to face the same problems (and some new ones, too) with new mates. In dealing with the pain of divorce and facing problems in new marriages, some of these couples seemed to change for the better and make good second marriages. But more than one had said, "If we had known earlier what we learned about solving problems in the second marriage, we might have been able to work out the problems in our first marriage."

Just before Carl told Karen about the other woman, he had called a professional counselor he knew. Carl told the counselor his life was out of control and he needed help. A few days before she found out about the affair, Karen had also gone to see a counselor because of her great distress.

Now they agreed to work at counseling separately and work hard with each other using what they had learned. They figured they would eventually get to a place where they could continue the marriage on a new agreed-upon basis *or* agree to terminate the marriage and be better prepared for a marriage with someone else.

In spite of the pain, confusion, and feelings of rejection, Carl and Karen were making some mature decisions: Both committed themselves to working on the marriage until they could figure out where they were. They both began counseling. They didn't make any hasty decisions about immediate divorce. Nobody moved out, and nobody took off their wedding rings.

What they had done, they realized later, was to individually make a deliberate, free-will commitment to each other and the marriage. Even though the problems weren't solved and no decision had yet been made, the steps they were taking were a lot different than those they had taken before marriage when they had assumed they would live "happily ever after." They had been wrong to think the wedding ceremony was somehow a guarantee. Already they had made progress.

As Carl's counseling continued, his "frantic plea" prayers changed to prayer for growth. He realized he would have to look at several areas of his life—the person who was Carl Abbott—and make some changes before he could expect to successfully rebuild his marriage. He began to learn *why* he functioned like he did. This process, though painful, was a revelation!

One area was his relationship with women in general. Even though he had broken off the affair with the other woman, Carl had a terrible fear that he would somehow become sexually involved again with another woman. He didn't understand how he'd gotten into an affair in the first place; maybe it would happen again, even though he didn't want it to! Then one day his counselor said, "Carl, you flirt with women and gamble with such a thing happening because you mistake sexual titillation or arousal in your interaction with women for acceptance of yourself as a person."

It was as if a heavy curtain opened in that moment, and sunlight streamed in. "For the first time I realized that was exactly what I was doing," Carl says, "and that I really didn't need that mistaken sense of acceptance from women."

That moment of healing insight was also spiritually significant for Carl. "God had not abandoned me. I could literally feel Christ's presence working through that professional counselor, opening my eyes and teaching me new behavioral skills so I could continue to grow on my own. Driving home from the counselor's office that day, I felt as though an enormous burden I had been carrying was gone. It was almost exhilarating—a wonderful relief from the negative feelings that had been dominating me for so long."

Carl also says, "Most important was a new seed of hope! I knew I would have to dig around in other crummy areas of my life; but in the process I knew I would grow personally and also be getting closer to a satisfying marriage relationship with Karen."

That insight became a key for understanding some other important misconceptions that affected Carl's relationships in general and his relationship with Karen in particular.

To understand why he needed that constant reassurance that he was loved and accepted, Carl and the counselor had to work back to his family of origin—his relationship with his parents.

"Did you know that your parents loved you?"

"Yes . . . no . . . I mean, sometimes I wasn't sure."

"Why was that?"

"I was afraid that if I wasn't good enough, my mother would leave me."

"What made you think that?"

"Because sometimes when I did something wrong, my mother would get very angry and tell me she was going to send me to an orphanage and leave me there."

"Which didn't happen."

"No, but . . . I've always had a fear that people I'm close to are going to reject me."

"And Karen?"

"Yes. Maybe especially Karen. Underneath, I guess I've always been afraid Karen might leave me. So I kept testing her love—would she respond to me sexually today? I had this terrible urge to control our marriage, to make sure Karen's love was still there."

"And if Karen responded?"

"I felt reassured that she still loved me."

"And if she didn't?"

"My fears were reinforced; maybe she didn't love me and might leave me."

Carl learned that he created his own fears—not Karen or any other person— and that he could learn, with practice, to not only understand but also control those fears. "Bringing my fears into the open, understanding where they came from, and being able to talk about them has been a wonderful and freeing experience for me," Carl says. "I have come a long way toward getting rid of those fears altogether, which has helped a great deal in healing our relationship."

Another seed of hope took root and sprouted.

Another "crummy area" that Carl had to face was an unconscious view of women which gave him "ownership rights" toward his wife.

"Accepting that Karen was a separate individual, with needs, responses, likes, and dislikes that were different than mine *and were OK* was a surprisingly difficult step for me," Carl says. "When I finally recognized it, it was as if another curtain opened, and I could clearly see what was on the other side. I experienced the presence of the Lord in that insight into myself and my way of thinking. I believe that's one way God works in our lives. I felt that same involvement of the Lord when I communicated my discovery to Karen and sensed her relief at my efforts to change that bias."

In the meantime, what was happening with Karen? No marriage crisis is one-sided. We each bring our strengths and limitations to a relationship. How those strengths and limitations interact is all part of the marriage dance that we struggle to learn. The goal, of course, is to learn to dance together in harmony with the music.

Karen kept her weekly appointments with the counselor for well over a year. "And I continue to talk with him even now," she says, "when I need an objective listener who not only can listen but can give me direction and knowledgeable advice."

After a counseling session, Karen and Carl would go home and talk and talk and talk—usually from nine or ten at night until two in the morning. As they shared their feelings, they came to believe the statement that "Feelings are neither right nor wrong; feelings are feelings." They struggled to understand the other person's point of view and accept each other—even when they didn't understand. "We cried a lot and laughed sometimes, too," Karen says. "We worked very hard at learning to communicate for the first time in our

married lives on a meaningful and realistic level."

Gradually Karen began to develop a
more realistic perspective on life, family,
and relationships. "I know now that our
son's alcohol and drug problems were
not 'my fault,'" she says. "I replaced the
old black-sheep-equals-parents'-fault
idea with a new lesson: I am responsible
for myself and nobody else; I am responsible *to* other people. I use this lesson
daily, especially in being responsible *to*,
but not responsible *for*, our two teenage
daughters. Our son is twenty-six years
old now; he has been to a treatment
center. He is a 'recovering' person, recovering from the disease of alcoholism
and other chemical dependencies. *He*
must do it; I can't do it for him."

Karen also came to accept that *life is
difficult* and that problems and pain are
a part of life. "Everybody has problems," she realized. "I don't have to hide
mine!"

What about the sexual tensions that
had plagued their relationship over the
years? Wouldn't any husband feel rejected and angry if his wife always ex-

pressed annoyance or disgust when he tried to turn her on?

"It was hard to talk about this," she says. "It seemed so obvious to me: getting sexy in the kitchen was bad timing. The kids were expecting dinner in half an hour, for goodness' sake! Why couldn't he leave me alone?

"And it wasn't just the kitchen. One day we were both out working in the yard; I was bending over in the garden. He came riding up on the power mower and swatted me on the behind! He rode off laughing—he thought it was funny. I didn't think it was funny; I felt used, just the butt of a joke."

But the long talks began to bear fruit. For the first time in their marriage, Karen realized that Carl's sex play didn't necessarily mean that he wanted to go to bed right then.

"I always thought it was all or nothing. If I encouraged him, I'd have to drop everything. So I kept him at arm's length until I thought the time was proper."

As Carl was able to verbalize his need for assurance and acceptance, Karen realized that for Carl sex was the "fix" when he didn't feel good. She began to understand why he felt so rejected when she didn't respond to his advances.

None of this happened overnight. For a long time hope seemed very far away. However, a deep love for each other—still there underneath the pain and confusion—kept the flicker of hope alive. Eventually that hope became like the blooming of a flower shown in slow-motion photography. The bud of hope was there, but it was tightly closed; then the flower grew as each petal unfolded in its own way—slowly and carefully uncurling to show the beauty and intricate detail of the blossom.

Soon after Carl and Karen began professional counseling, they also became deeply involved in a church renewal movement called Cursillo. "In that group of Christians," Karen says, "I have learned to love, to be vulnerable, to risk letting others know the real me. That includes saying how I feel and admitting I have problems. I have been enveloped in the reality that we can share each other's burdens. Sharing eases the pain and encourages growth. Learning to do that with people I care about and who care about me has helped me do that in my relationship with Carl."

Both Carl and Karen were learning some valuable insights:

- *I sometimes mistake how others respond to me with acceptance of myself as a person.*
- *Fears of rejection can cause me to constantly test whether I am loved, creating unhealthy tensions.*
- *My spouse is not just an extension of myself but a separate individual with needs, responses, likes, and dislikes that may differ from mine.*
- *Everybody has problems; I don't have to hide mine.*
- *Feelings are neither right nor wrong; feelings are feelings.*
- *I am responsible for myself and nobody else; I am responsible to other people.*

What can we do with these insights?

Let's look at how Carl and Karen acted on their new vision.

Making a conscious decision that Karen's responsiveness to his spur-of-the-moment sexual advances did not equal her acceptance of him as a person, Carl was able to give up trying to control their sexual relationship. "I immediately sensed a change in Karen," Carl marvels. "She seemed to begin enjoying our physical relationship in a new way."

Karen adds, "We learned to meet each other halfway. As Carl realized he didn't need constant sexual reassurance that I loved and accepted him, he was able to be more sensitive to my needs. And as I sensed him accepting me as an individual person, with feelings and needs that were different from his but were OK, I felt able to give more sexually—because I wanted to, not because he was demanding it."

Does Carl feel satisfied? "I am generally happy and satisfied with our sexual life at this point. More important, however, I don't have that unhealthy need to control Karen sexually to assure me she loves me. I still have to work on that problem but . . . that's OK as long as I am working on it!"

Learning to see Karen as an independent, separate person with whom he is in partnership in their marriage has had "an added blessing," Carl says. "I have been able to consciously model a healthier male person for our two teenage daughters and help them see themselves as equal children of God. Karen and I both talk with the girls about what we have learned in our marriage relationship and how they can apply those skills in relationships they now have and will have in the future with people of both sexes."

Do the Abbotts now have the perfect marriage that eluded them before? Carl shakes his head. "It's easy for either or both of us to 'backslide' to old behaviors and 'replay old tapes' in areas where we're changing. But when we do, it's easier now to see what we're doing and to talk about what's happening. In that way, we not only regroup to the place of growth, but in the process we grow a little more and secure our relationship a little more."

With the advantage of counseling, both Carl and Karen are keenly aware of marriage dynamics and their feelings, which are the key to understanding those dynamics. They now have an agreement—which they honor—to quickly and gently point out to the other what each is feeling and what they think about problems that arise. They now either talk through the feelings or work out the problems to the satisfaction of both.

With hard work and practice, they have learned how to deal with and resolve problems and life issues that affect the marriage relationship without threatening the relationship. Because of this, they believe that as individuals and as a couple they are continually growing stronger.

Karen also believes her personal faith and trust in God has made her marriage struggle survivable. A friend of the Abbotts once described faith this way: "When you are at the end of your rope, tie a knot and hang on!"

"I have hung on," Karen says, "and Carl has hung on, too. I see us now as individuals who are *choosing* to be married to each other." She grins a pixie grin.

"That rope we were hanging onto for dear life has become more like a swing moving between life's problems and pains and its joys and laughter. Swings go up . . . swings go down. It's all part of the ride. With faith, I'm enjoying the ride more all the time."

CHAPTER THREE

But Is He Trustworthy?

The doorbell rang three times before Esther Bishop could answer it, and then she was surprised to see two police officers standing there.

"Mrs. Bishop?" one asked, and Esther nodded. "Is your husband home?"

"Well, yes. He just got home from work."

"Would you mind if we came in? We'd like to talk to him for a few minutes."

"I suppose so," Esther said as she swung open the door. "Is there some problem?"

"We'd just like to talk to your husband."

Esther's mind was a whirl as she went to call Kurt from the backyard.

When Kurt came in, tall and muscular in contrast to his auburn-haired, petite wife, he looked at the police officers in surprise. "Uh, sit down," he said. "How can I help you?"

Once all four people were seated in the living room, the younger policeman asked Kurt, "I wonder if you could tell us where you were last evening at about ten-forty-five?"

"I . . . well, I was at home, I think. Let's see . . . I went out to fill the car with gas right after dinner, but then I came back and watched TV until we went to bed at about eleven o'clock. Yeah. I had to be at home at ten-forty-five."

Esther's heart was thumping hard. Maybe Kurt just didn't remember correctly, but it had been the other way around. He had watched TV after dinner and left the house at about nine-thirty. She didn't know where he went, but when he came in around eleven o'clock, he seemed upset and wouldn't even speak to her. Even then the familiar fear had skittered across the back of her mind that maybe it was all starting again. He had been so moody the last few days.

"Where'd you go today?" the officer asked.

"Just to work and back," Kurt said. "Why? What are all these questions about, anyway?"

"If you just went to work and back, then your car would still be nearly full of gas, wouldn't it? Mind if we have a look?"

"Well, I didn't actually fill it up. I only had five bucks in my pocket. So that's all I put in. It probably won't register full."

"Mr. Bishop," the older policeman broke in, "last evening there was a Peeping Tom reported in the neighborhood. The description of the suspect seems to fit you awfully closely. Are you sure you were home at ten-forty-five?"

"Absolutely. I was in bed by eleven o'clock. Wasn't I, Esther?"

Esther froze. How could he involve her in his filthy little games? Could he have really stooped so low? And why hadn't she been able to stop him? But before she realized it, she heard herself saying, "Yes, we were in bed by eleven o'clock."

"Thank you. That will be all for now." The officers stood and started for the door. "However, if you should remember anything else from last night, Mr. Bishop, it might be a good idea to give us a call, OK?"

"Sure will," Kurt said as he let them out. When he returned he avoided Esther's eyes.

Esther didn't take shocks like this very easily. Although she had grown up in a Christian home and remembers her childhood as a happy time, she struggled with low self-esteem. Normal teenage insecurity seemed to increase the competition she felt with her older sister. Feeling like she couldn't measure up, Esther sometimes did things just to be "different," not always meeting parental approval. Conflict with her mother escalated. She felt self-conscious about her freckles, sprinkled generously across her face under the cap of auburn hair. She dated very little and lacked confidence in herself. And when she quit college in the middle of her junior year, she knew her family was disappointed.

When dating picked up in college, her "need to be needed" caused her to take each relationship too seriously. When each one ended, she was usually the one to get hurt.

But, she recalls, when she met Kurt it was excitingly different. "We hit it off so quickly. On our first date we sat up all night just talking, nothing physical. How good and refreshing it felt to be able to share with someone so easily."

Kurt and Esther were married one year later, and the first year was fun and fulfilling. In their second year Kurt was transferred to Las Vegas—a long way from their small home town in Illinois.

"There we were in a big city, in unfamiliar surroundings, with no family and friends . . . and Kurt began to tell me some of the problems he'd been having," Esther says. "He told me that he'd been going to some bars with topless dancers, to massage parlors, and to X-rated movies. I was really shocked by his confessions and began to grill him with questions."

"I didn't understand it myself," recalls Kurt. "It started before we were married—pornography, peep shows—but I excused it as the kind of sexual drive that would be satisfied with marriage. The thing that troubled me was that I found myself doing the same things after we were married."

Kurt winces a bit behind his wire rim glasses. "I had taken my marriage vows seriously and really wanted to live by them. Yet I felt like I was continually breaking them, doing things I knew would hurt Esther if she ever found out. I felt like such a failure. I was sure that nobody else had ever experienced what I was experiencing and no one would understand if I tried to tell them. But finally, after a year and a half of marriage, I couldn't stand it any longer and confessed to Esther about my 'other life'."

The more Kurt told Esther, however, the more frightened she became—frightened because she was discovering that the person to whom she was married was not the person she thought she had married. Why hadn't he shared this with her before they were married? Would she have married him if she had known? How much more was to come out? An even scarier part was Kurt's tearful admissions that he didn't want to do these things, but he couldn't help it. Crying with him, she promised to help . . . but what could she do?

A whirlwind courtship, the excitement of being newlyweds . . . then, suddenly, the honeymoon is over. The dark side of personalities begins to show. Most couples experience this in one form or another—she in curlers, he unshaven. But some marriages are forced to face severe emotional problems, previously unsuspected. A spouse sees behaviors that don't make sense.

Bewildered and scared, the spouse gropes blindly for some rationale. Like an undiagnosed illness, the couple suffers both the pain of the experience and the frustration of the mystery.

When Kurt confessed his disturbing behavior, Esther made her own diagnosis:

"Kurt lacks self-control." In their own ways, both Kurt and Esther denied that this was a problem that needed "real" help. But without true understanding, knowing how to proceed was just a guess and a gamble.

Esther's way of "helping" was to become Kurt's watchdog, monitoring his comings and goings and everything he did. She also insisted on knowing all the details of his past. Kurt didn't know why she wanted all the particulars, but he developed a private theory: the more she knew, the more she could hold over his head to show him what a bad person he was. In self-defense, Kurt began to blame Esther for not being sexual enough to take care of his "needs."

On the surface, things seemed to go OK. Kurt's Las Vegas assignment ended, and they were able to move back home among friends. Certainly being out of the big city would remove some of the temptations, they reasoned. They got involved at their church as youth sponsors and taught Sunday school. But there were times when Kurt was withdrawn and quiet. When Esther started probing, Kurt would finally confess something he had done—a porno movie or a topless bar. This happened again and again: Kurt confessing, Esther crying, Kurt apologizing.

Emotionally, Esther was a mess. She began doubting herself, thinking she was to blame. "I felt inadequate as a wife, both emotionally and sexually," she recalls. "If I were a good wife, I thought, Kurt wouldn't be doing these things."

Slowly her confidence was sinking lower and lower. She resigned as a manager at her job and took another position because she couldn't handle the pressure of people and problems at work and the struggle with her marriage at home. She began to have nightmares where she was all alone and no one wanted or liked her.

She became depressed and cried a lot, calling in sick to work because she couldn't face the day. The whole time she kept the secret from family and friends, never sharing it with anyone. How could she? Who in the world would understand what was happening to them? What would they think of Kurt?

"I felt like I was wearing a costume," Esther says. "My family and friends related to the costume, not to the lonely, hurting person inside. Partly I prayed that no one would see beyond the costume; partly I yearned for someone to do just that."

Kurt was equally isolated. "My predominant feeling was numbness," he recalls. "I felt as if I were outside looking in at myself but couldn't touch me. The worst part was how things kept going in unbreakable cycles." It was never long after a confession before his activities would start up again: peep shows, massage parlors, pornography, X-rated movies. And of course with each episode there were lies, deception, guilt, and the fear of being caught.

What made this time confusing was that they did have good times together, too. "Kurt is naturally gentle and thoughtful," Esther says of the man she married. "He has a great sense of humor, and we enjoy laughing together. But I felt like a ball being tossed back and forth. In one glove I was happy, secure, and loved; in the other glove I was scared, lonely, depressed. I kept being tossed back and forth and didn't seem to have any control over my life."

Kurt also felt out of control. "The feelings of failure and hopelessness were so great that I could hardly face myself, let alone Esther or anyone else," recalls Kurt. What neither of them could understand was how Kurt could keep on hurting Esther and their marriage if he loved her and wanted to be married.

Esther and Kurt fell into a common marital trap. Esther's focus shifted from monitoring her own life to monitoring Kurt's. She absorbed the responsibility for his aberrant behavior. It was up to her to make sure he didn't act out his addiction. When she failed in her objective, she felt responsible. As the pressure on her increased, she tried to gain more control. As her supervision intensified, he reacted to her rather than face his own issues.

No spouse can "fix" the other, though

this is a typical response when couples run into problems. It is one way a spouse "enables" a loved one with compulsive behavior to avoid taking responsibility for his own behavior.

The Peeping Tom incident was the last straw for Esther. Kurt may have gotten the police to leave, but Esther knew he had been the Peeping Tom. And Kurt knew that she knew.

"When did you do this?"

"You heard 'em. Last night."

"But what time?"

"When I went out. I didn't go get any gas."

"Where'd you go, then?"

"Just down the block."

"Down the block, where?" Again Esther probed for details, frantically trying to understand and keep in control.

"Why?" she cried desperately. "Why do you keep doing these things? Don't you know it's destroying me, our marriage?"

Of course there was never an answer to *why*. "All I knew," remembers Kurt, "was that I hated myself and what I was doing. But it seemed that a force I couldn't resist was in control of my life most of the time."

Finally, Esther gave up her questioning. "Kurt," she said, "we can't go on like this anymore. We have to get help. I'm going to call our minister." Kurt didn't resist.

The minister came right over and talked with Kurt and Esther well into the night. When he left, he promised to make appointments for them with a private counselor. As the door finally shut behind him, Esther felt a sense of relief. The secret was out.

We can only wear a mask so long. Taking off our masks allows a new perspective. Sharing our struggles gives opportunity for outside support. When one or both spouses say "Something has to change," a first step has been taken. Some despair lifts when we no longer feel we are going it alone.

Like a reoccurring headache, people in pain usually settle for relief of the symptoms rather than a cure. Neither Kurt nor Esther understood that Kurt's compul-

sions were his attempt to seek relief from a deep inner pain. They both believed that the absence of the behavior was the absence of the problem. They didn't understand that without a clear diagnosis and understanding of the problem, the symptoms will always reappear.

Esther did the right thing to call for help. Seeking help for marital troubles should be as natural as visiting the family doctor about an illness. It was only the first step of a long journey, but the first step always needs to be taken.

Engaging a counselor didn't seem to come in time for Esther. She had lost all trust in Kurt, and she poured all her energy into making it difficult for him to go anywhere without her. "I made sure he never had any free time or free money to pursue his sexual highs," she admits.

But being a mother hen was not compatible with being a wife. Furthermore, Esther's obsession with brooding over everything Kurt did also meant that she had fewer activities and friends of her own, which she soon began to resent.

Her lack of freedom and preoccupation with "Kurt's problem" was not what she wanted in a marriage. Should she leave him? But she decided she couldn't do that. "I loved him and decided to do all I could to help him change and conquer *his* problem," Esther says.

They stopped the counseling after several months because, according to Kurt, everything was going OK. Esther agreed to terminate, partly because she was so tired of dealing with the situation. She just wanted it to be over, even though she still didn't trust him.

Then, while Kurt was away on business, Esther developed severe lower abdominal pains and immediately underwent surgery for a tubal pregnancy. When she was first told she was pregnant, she felt a rush of happiness. But within a short time, the joy was crushed, knowing she would lose the baby. It was a real blow. Her minister and a few friends visited her in the hospital, but she still felt very alone.

Kurt did not rush back, and when he did arrive a few days later and tried to cheer her up, Esther was disappointed at his reaction to the loss. "It was a medical crisis, and I lost my baby, but Kurt's way of consoling me was to downplay the whole thing. He treated me like I was just overreacting," says Esther.

Then, several months later—just after their sixth anniversary, actually—Kurt sat Esther down one night and said, "This just isn't working. You are on me all the time. It's as though you expect me to do something wrong."

"I don't *expect* you to do something wrong, Kurt. But I still don't feel very secure with you. I still don't know what you are doing half the time."

"What do you mean, you still don't know what I'm doing? You're on my back all the time."

"I am not. Like where'd you go last night? You just took off."

Kurt sat silently, staring at the floor for a long time. "Well . . . I might as well tell you. I *am* seeing someone else. That's where I was last night."

"You're *what?*"

"I said I'm seeing someone else. Look, I don't want this constant tension any more, so I think it would be best for us to separate."

Esther felt like she'd been hit head-on by a truck. She couldn't move. She couldn't believe what she'd heard. Separate? She knew they still had problems, but she never thought Kurt would leave her.

Unable to think clearly, she left the house and stayed with a friend. After several days, Esther realized that she needed her familiar surroundings. "I couldn't stand the idea of Kurt bringing someone else into *my* house," Esther remembers. "And, since the separation was *his* choice, I figured he ought to be the one to move out."

Kurt did move out, reinforcing himself with the notion that he was tired of all the lies and deception to get around Esther. He thought he wanted to be free to seek sexual experiences whenever and wherever he wanted. But the separation didn't bring the freedom he imagined.

"Suddenly I was alone," he says, "alienated from many of my friends and cut off from much of what had been an important part of my normal life. I re-member shortly after we separated, I saw an old man sweeping his porch. I realized that if I weren't careful, I could end up a lonely old man, spending the rest of my life by myself.

"As for my sexual thrills, they weren't all that great. I still wasn't happy or satisfied. Slowly I began to feel like I wasn't a good enough person to deserve Esther's love or be able to return that love to her. I didn't want to see her or even be around her because there was always so much hurt on her face."

The pain was more than a mask on Esther's face. She couldn't sleep at night. She began losing weight because she couldn't keep food down. She went driving at night, contemplating crashing her car. She quit going to church because she didn't want to talk to people; she felt like an outcast who didn't fit in anywhere. Her sense of failure stirred the old feeling that, once again, she had disappointed her parents.

Her self-esteem withering, Esther withdrew further and further from those who were trying to help her.

Friends would ask her to do things, but she'd make up excuses to stay home. All she really wanted was to be with Kurt, but he didn't want to be with her.

When Kurt and Esther did get together to talk about the bills or the house, Esther felt Kurt was snappy, mean, and hurtful—an entirely different person than she'd known before. He never mentioned divorce, yet she felt he could hardly look at her and be civil.

When she appealed to her minister and mutual friends to make Kurt change his mind, however, they just said, "Let him alone; Kurt needs to be left alone."

Esther felt confused. How could that be? Certainly *he* was in the wrong and needed to change, so why were they suggesting that he be left alone?

What is happening here?

Everything Esther tried has backfired. She tried to "help" Kurt by making it difficult for him to indulge in his sexual activities; she insisted they get help. But nothing really changed; in fact, now Kurt had left her!

*Everything Kurt has done has back-
fired, too. He shared his problems with
Esther and only got unrelenting suspicion
and pain in return. He tried to get out of
the situation and just "accept" himself,
but the guilt and dissatisfaction wouldn't
go away.*

*Unfortunately, the "watchdog" role Es-
ther took on herself actually hindered
Kurt from dealing with his problem. His
focus became trying to get around Esther's
stranglehold; she was actually "enabling"
Kurt to continue his behavior.*

*When a spouse is struggling with com-
pulsive behavior, the first thing the enabler
must do is stand back and let consequences happen.*

Though frustrated, Esther quit chasing
after Kurt. With the support of a few
close friends and her minister, she began taking a long, slow look at herself.
It dawned on her that she had depended
exclusively on Kurt for her happiness
and fulfillment. Without Kurt around,
she began to take hold of herself, become more independent, and work at

becoming the kind of a person she could be proud of.

She did simple, symbolic things like buy new clothes, begin exercising, and go out with friends. She also turned to her Bible more, and found that she could depend on God in ways she should never expect from Kurt. And the words of a song kept going through her mind, giving her special strength: "God makes everything beautiful, in His time."

"I wanted everything to be beautiful *now*," she remembers. "But those words and the prayers of lots of friends were giving me insight and the hope that God had something special for me . . . if I'd be patient."

Slowly the changes inside began to have outward expression. When she was with Kurt, she found that she could be positive and cheerful instead of the crying, begging, pitiful person she had been.

One day, Kurt told Esther that he had gone to a counselor for help. Did she dare hope? Were her prayers beginning to be answered? There was a difference:

This time Kurt was getting help on his own without her prodding and pushing. He had gone to the counselor, not because of her pressure, but because he had hit bottom.

"Bottom" for Kurt was not a crisis, but the slow, sure realization that he couldn't go on the way it was. Separation had not solved his problems or brought him sexual satisfaction. The "other woman" had moved out of town, and Kurt saw clearly that the cycles of sexual titillation, guilt, and remorse just kept repeating themselves. On a slow, rainy day at work, he realized he was utterly powerless to change without help.

When a person is in the grip of an addiction, realizing one is powerless to change without help is essential. For many, the darkest hour really is before the dawn.

As parents, spouses, and loved ones, we hate to see learning take place in the "school of hard knocks." But unwittingly we only delay recovery by protecting the addict from the full reality of the consequences of his behavior. Once at the bot-

*tom, the addict needs repentance, humil-
ity, and admission of the need for help, all
important keys to recovery.*

Whatever Kurt expected, he was surprised when the counselor told him that
his abnormal, deviant behavior was the
result of depression. His first reaction
was disbelief. He had never thought of
himself as the kind of person who sits
around all day with his head in his
hands, and indeed that was not the way
he expressed or dealt with depression.

"Are you *sure* depression is the root
of my actions?" asked Kurt one day as
he finished a counseling session.

"Yes," the counselor assured him.
"People deal with depression in a lot of
ways. *You* cope with depression by seeking sexual thrills, which has become—
literally—a sexual addiction. But in
order to deal with your sexual addiction, you will need to first deal with the
depression."

Strangely, Kurt left the counselor's office with a spring in his step. "Sexual
addiction"—that was scary. But there
was also a relief in putting a name on the

force that had been ruining his life and marriage. The fact that there seemed to be a reason relieved Kurt of the feeling that he was just a "bad" person. The counselor told him that there would be a lot of work ahead, but change *was* possible. What a relief!

Slowly, Kurt began to understand what had been happening to him. He explains it this way: "As I look back on my life, I realize that I spent many years suffering from depression, even though I didn't know it at the time. During my teen years I did all the right things because that was what was expected. The trouble was that no matter how 'good' I was, I just wasn't ever happy or at peace with myself.

"When I was twenty, I discovered a 'high' that took away the depression for little bits of time: masturbation. This soon led to a cycle of depression, then anticipation of and activities leading up to the act of masturbating. There would be the momentary high, then I'd be right back into guilt and disgust with myself, and then back into the depression. In short, I was a sexual addict caught up in a never-ending cycle.

"For many people, masturbation is part of perfectly normal adolescent development. But for me it became an addiction, a behavior I used to try to push back the depression—ineffective though it was. As time went on, I extended my masturbation to other sexual highs in an ever widening circle to find longer-lasting relief from my depression. And my addiction didn't change when I got married because it wasn't really a sexual outlet that I was needing. Therefore, in marriage my addiction just became more complicated."

Esther also began seeing a counselor at the same place where Kurt was getting help. Her initial objective was to work at becoming more the kind of person *she* could love and thereby improve her sense of self-worth. But she also hoped to discover more about Kurt's problem so she could be more helpful to him.

Initially, it was scary to discover that he had an addiction with many of the dynamics of a chemical addiction—

something he would have to deal with the rest of his life. But it was a relief to know that they were dealing with an illness and one that could be managed.

However, the thing that really surprised Esther was the discovery that she had been a "co-addict" to Kurt's problem. As it turned out, all the time she thought she was protecting him by monitoring his behavior, she was actually feeding it. Her controlling, "helping" attitude was actually making it worse by insulating Kurt from the raw nature and consequences of his addiction.

Though confusing and painful at first, these new revelations were very helpful to Esther. She had always thought that if Kurt would just quit what he was doing, everything would be OK; she discovered it wasn't that simple. In some ways that was reassuring. His failure to stop his behavior did not mean that he was deliberately trying to hurt her.

Kurt and Esther were learning some valuable facts:

- *Self-esteem based on how others respond to us can leave us very insecure. Receiving our sense of self-worth from our Creator and accepting ourselves as we are with all our strengths and weaknesses gives us the only firm foundation.*
- *We are each responsible for ourselves and to others. But we are not responsible for the behavior of other adults—even our spouse.*
- *Emotional problems sometimes have unusual expressions. Conversely, unusual behavior may have complicated roots, making it hard, if not impossible, to "just stop."*
- *While true addictions are not curable, they are manageable for those who admit the problem, accept help, and remain accountable for their behavior.*
- *It is important to foster patience. Most important changes take time.*

With individual counseling nurturing the seeds of insight and hope, Kurt and Esther began "dating" again and actually having fun together. But Esther still cried herself to sleep at night, partly out of loneliness and partly because she was confused about how she really felt. She knew that she still loved Kurt and wanted to be with him . . . yet she worried whether she was strong enough to live with his illness. Could she really change the way she worried and watched him? It had become a habit for her.

"My thoughts and feelings were playing tug-of-war," she says. "One side would say, 'You love him and that's what is important.' Then the other side would say, 'Yes, but can you trust him? Are you willing to risk being hurt again? Can you really forgive him for the affair and the hurt you went through?'"

Still, Esther kept seeing Kurt more often until it became a daily occurrence. Then they began marriage counseling together.

Part of that counseling had to deal with the pain of what had happened. There was now an explanation for Kurt's behavior that made it more understandable; he hadn't been doing it to hurt Esther or because he didn't love her. But it had still hurt. His behavior had been a break of trust and commitment, especially when he became involved with another woman. It wasn't easy to take responsibility for the pain it had caused Esther, but Kurt repented and asked for her forgiveness. It took time, but Esther was able to extend full forgiveness.

After eight months of separation, Kurt moved back home. Esther recalls that they had some significant adjustments to make because both of them had changed. She had more confidence in herself and had gained some self-esteem. Coming back together seemed like the first year of their marriage all over again. Only this time they knew each other better and had better communication skills. They used the skills they had learned in counseling together in two ways: first, to heal the hurts of the past, and second, to give them tools for the future. "I don't see counseling as a one-time thing," Kurt says. "We may need to use it again as our relationship grows."

Through counseling, Esther learned

that for their relationship to work, she needed to *let go* of Kurt. He was responsible for himself; he was not her responsibility. In the past she had tried to control and protect him from his behavior. Now she needed to give total freedom.

To work at this, she purposely planned evenings away with her friends. Although at first those times were short, it gradually became easier. During their separation she had developed some new friendships and interests which she continued to build on once she and Kurt were reconciled. And she found herself enjoying the new freedom of not playing "mother" or "watchdog." She also found that the more freedom she gave Kurt, the more openly he shared his feelings and activities with her.

One of the things Kurt appreciated most was Esther's new willingness to become involved in a recreation he enjoyed: fishing. "Not only does it show me that I am important to her, but it has provided many quiet hours together and a chance to try our new communication skills when things aren't going so well."

And when Kurt quit trying to make sex fulfill a need for which it was never intended, he discovered that Esther had no lack of sexual interest and enjoyed their intimate times as much as he did.

Now the problems were falling into perspective. Strategies were working. Kurt was working on his response to periodic depression. Esther was working on her response to a shaky self-esteem. Understanding was growing in each person and in the relationship. Trust in self and each other was building.

Endless time and energy spent pushing/pulling, crawling/running, was now being channeled into positive, life-generating activity. As Kurt and Esther were learning, the recovery process doesn't leave couples "OK" for the moment. Rather, it puts them on track for a truly enriched relationship.

Kurt and Esther realized they needed to rebuild not only their marriage but also their relationship with others as a couple. They began to attend church together again and to associate with their church friends.

Shortly after they moved back together, Kurt shared his story with the congregation on a Sunday morning. That may seem unusually bold, but it was an important time of healing, forgiveness, and renewal for both him and Esther. They had lived too long with secrets, pretending to be one thing while living a lie. In order to live openly and honestly with one another, they needed to own and accept the past, as painful as it had been.

To help them do this, the Bishops also continue to be involved in a marriage support group at church. It serves as a sounding board for problems and possible solutions. And it has been helpful to realize that they're not the only couple who have struggles.

Kurt continues to take medication to help control his depression. The medication is a great help, but it doesn't mean that he never gets depressed. But he and Esther have both learned that times of depression *will pass*, and it seems to work for both of them to just ride them out rather than try to solve them. Kurt's challenge is to be constantly alert that he doesn't slip into his old habits when he has bad days.

Now that they have two small children, Esther and Kurt are discovering a whole new set of joys, smiles, and loves—as well as frustrations and problems! Time for each other doesn't come as easily as before the children arrived. It is a real struggle to find the time to get away as a couple and have fun just being together. But they realize that even though it has been seven years since their reconciliation, they need to make time for each other for their relationship to work.

Esther also has to continually work at trusting Kurt and letting go of him. "Sometimes I find myself reverting back to my old behavior of wanting to control—especially when he gets home later than I expected," she reports.

But what they prayed for did happen. They are rebuilding their marriage, step by step, year by year, with hope and laughter thrown in. Not in their own time, but in God's time.

CHAPTER FOUR

Can *You* Ever Trust Again?

The story is common: She discovered her husband was having an affair. He confessed and said he would stop. She believed she would never be able to trust, forgive, or love him again. They're now divorced, she's a single mother of three, he wants to rejoin the family. He says he's sorry; she says the pain and betrayal is too great.

How do we understand adultery?

We hear it whispered: "I think she's cheating on him." "He's got roaming eyes." "She's a tart." "People should just forgive and forget." "Spouses just aren't faithful to each other any more." "If I ever catch him with another woman, I'm gone." "There's no coming back."

"The Bible says I'm justified to leave."
"The Bible says I should stay."

If you're feeling a little overwhelmed, you are not alone. These are tough times for many couples. But don't despair! Strong marriages abound, we just have to find them. We just have to make them. The institution of marriage is as old as recorded time. There is much to learn—and many people to learn from.

The marital union exists as a bond blessed by God. As God relates to us, God hopes we will relate to each other, especially in marriage. Within the most sacred aspect of our being—our will, desires, and ultimate loyalty—God wants no other god.

Just as our relationship with God has a structure with expectations and boundaries, so does marriage. Just as our relationship with God is designed for abundant living, so is marriage. The rewards desperately longed for in marriage are only available within the design of God's union. But an intimate, lifelong partnership within marriage is difficult.

More Than an Affair

Some people think adultery is merely sex outside of marriage. But the deeper tragedy is a spiritual one. God's ideal for marriage involves total trust. Adultery results when something happens to trust. Marriage requires trusting that God's design is sufficient to meet the promise of the abundant life every new bride and groom hope for.

What we see in the stories of reconciled marriage is a recommitment to God and to each other. A building block for hope is found in the rekindling of the trust, and the hope is that the joy each spouse is looking for can be found *within* the marriage.

Reconciliation takes both sides. At times, one spouse may try harder (or seem to). One's effort may be more visible one day, the other the next. Eventually both partners participate.

Communication Expectations

As seen in the stories within this book, a key step was taken when the couples actively discussed their expectations. Couples who can sit down and talk about their feelings have taken the first step. Carl and Karen spent long hours gaining an understanding of what each of them were thinking and feeling. They established a goal: a mutual desire for living together in a healthy marriage.

For the sake of their marriage, they gave up believing they knew all the answers. Both accepted an openness to growth.

The healing of broken trust is *not* built on dreamy, star-struck romance. This time the couple bases their trust on the most comprehensive knowledge of another person one can ever obtain.

Depths of Forgiveness

Healing the broken trust that follows adultery requires granting forgiveness more deeply than most of us want to do. Is it possible to forgive as Christ forgave those who put Him to death? Can we receive forgiveness as Peter did following his betrayal of Christ? As the healing process unfolds, a multitude of sins by both spouses pour out. Adultery occurs in a context—not at random. Reconciling couples discover a mutual understanding of each other's humanness.

In time both see each other's pain. They learn to respect each other's struggle. Each partner takes responsibility for his or her own changes. But they also work at becoming a team.

The life stories in this book provide only a glimpse of the range of dysfunctional marriages. They hint at the endless variety of marriages in which trust is broken. They show a context where affairs often take place.

Messages

Emily Brown, a social worker who leads workshops for clinicians on affairs, identifies five messages that distinguish affairs. They are as follows:

1. *"Let's avoid conflict; I don't want to deal directly with my differences with you, but I do want you to pay attention to me."* In these situations, conflict is feared, discussion shuts down, and the road to intimacy is untraveled. But the walls designed to prevent conflict also prevent closeness. While an affair might temporarily feel like closeness, in reality

it merely pretends to provide the basic needs of emotional intimacy. Affairs feel like intimacy, but they are not. They are elusive fantasies.

2. *"Let's not get too close"* is another message. Extreme fear of intimacy strangles these marriages. Emotional intertwining is risky. Some spouses buffer closeness with affairs.

3. *"I need someone else to prove I'm wanted, that I'm OK."* Insatiable emotional emptiness may also drive affairs. Sex is used to try to reinforce self-esteem. Childhoods riddled with abuse can be a breeding ground for the sexual addict. The pain-filled foundations are built long before the marriage begins. Whether a womanizer or a seductress, the addict seeks but never finds. Again intimacy goes unfound.

4. *"Let's not work at it—it's just not worth it."* Some marriages begin well but are not maintained. Daily, weekly, and seasonal moments of celebration are the lifeblood of marriage. Unattended, a gradual emotional divorce occurs. When life gets lonely, there is no one to turn to. When pain comes, no marital haven ex-

ists. If opportunity avails itself, the temptation is too strong.

5. *"I'm really gone; I just haven't told you yet."* The affair is used as a convenient method of announcing that the person wants out of the relationship. Disregarding past or present, the affair carries the person from one bed to another.

But while these downward pulls of life are strong, and the recipes for despair seem endless, the road to reconciliation does have some clear markings.

Repairing

Healing broken trust demands a one-two punch. Behaviors must change, and beliefs must be revised. Talking is never enough. Similarly, actions without understanding are inadequate.

The hurtful moments in marriage are experienced in a myriad of ways. But the stages that most couples go through in the healing process can be outlined.

1. Acknowledge the trouble and its severity.
2. Make a joint commitment to work for health.

3. Agree to try.
4. Stop the blaming.
5. Conduct a self-examination.
6. Seek help to understand the negative interactions.
7. Embrace a new way of living.
8. Celebrate growth.

Healing begins when people acknowledge that there is a serious problem. Let's look at the steps along the way.

Step on a nail. Touch a hot stove. In an instant the whole body is aware that something is wrong. But in a marriage little hurts come daily. Like the body's nervous system, marriage partners need a way to acknowledge when something is wrong. Too often communication channels become garbled. Anger or blame confuses pain messages. Haven't you noticed that it is much easier to get angry or blame the other person than to simply say you are hurting? Sometimes it is just too humiliating to say, "I'm hurting." It's as though admitting it is to admit weakness, and that's the last thing we want to do when we feel we are down.

Therefore, hurts are held inside. In each couple's story, remember the points where the pain was acknowledged by both.

Next came a commitment to each other and to mutual health. Out of estrangement and confusion, one agreement was reached: "We want to be healthy." It may seem like a small thing, but it is really a big step forward.

At this point most couples believe they have been expending energy to help the marriage, and they may feel too tired to go on. But much of what they've tried has been futile. This happens because they haven't jointly agreed on the problem and how to work for a solution. Team work must be rediscovered. Blame must be eliminated. Self-examination now needs to happen. Rather than finding fault, each person must identify his or her participation in *the good and the bad* aspects of the marriage.

Each spouse must own his or her own humanness. In every interaction both partners have an opportunity to think and act in new ways. Marriages work best when the partners function as fans and encouragers of each other. It's dangerous to try to be the other person's coach and deadly to be the critic.

As each spouse matures, the questions to be asked change. "What should you do for me?" becomes "What can I do for you?" The question "Who's right or wrong?" is not as important as "How have we misunderstood each other?"

Rather than pushing and pulling each other around a dance floor, a gentle touch keeps the couple moving harmoniously.

Both keep a watchful eye for the appearance of old patterns. Previous success assures the couple that they can solve the current dilemma. With each repair the couple's hope builds—not because they are immune to hurt, but because they understand healing.

As fears of change are conquered, the rewards of personal and marital growth are experienced. A marriage riddled with despair and dysfunction can be renewed and come alive. Each life struggle sets the stage for a potential celebration.

Prevention

Do really bad things have to happen before couples work at marriage? Of course not! Like a machine, steady maintenance protects.

Repairing brokenness daily is a foundational principle for marital problem prevention. TV, magazines, talk around town—these are not often very supportive of marriage. When conflicts arise, the world is so quick to take sides. Couples pursuing healthy relationships need to spend time with other couples who are also committed to health. Role models of a healthy marriage need to be found. Good marriages are not random occurrences, they are intentional.

To keep your own marriage strong, trust yourself enough to be in touch with your thoughts and feelings. Trust your spouse enough to share them. The pull of temptation thrives on secrecy. Don't underestimate its influence. In his book, *Hedges*, Jerry Jenkins suggests several rules for protecting your marriage. You may have to read his book to see their full wisdom, but consider this paraphrased summary:

1. Whenever meeting or dining with an unrelated person of the opposite sex, make it a threesome.

2. Be careful about touching. A handshake is usually adequate. An embrace in private is foolish.

3. If you pay a compliment, do not direct it to one's personal beauty or handsomeness, but to the clothes.

4. Avoid flirtation or suggestive conversation, even in jest.

5. Rehearse your wedding vows often to your spouse: "Keeping you only unto me for as long as we both shall live . . ."

6. Do not let your work rob your relationship of its quality or priority. Don't bring work home.[1]

Don't underestimate your marriage's resiliency either. When temptation arises, work at overcoming embarrassment, shame, and fear. Identify the root cause. How is this temptation tricking me? For what problem do I believe it to be a solution? What "fix" is available? What can I do to avoid the guilt, self-destructiveness, and harm to others which follows giving into temptation?

The tragedy temptation brings is prevented when solutions are pleasing to self, spouse, and God.

Farewell

The true stories you have read in this book are gifts of love. Love made them possible. Love caused them to be told.

The Recovery of Hope movement is made up of couples who care about marriages. They care about hurting spouses because they've all been one. Let their stories be a gift of hope, an act of love, and a sacred trust that God's reconciling power will be available to you each day.

CHAPTER FIVE

What Is Recovery of Hope?

Recovery of Hope (ROH) is a program for couples who are experiencing disillusionment in their marriages. Some may be contemplating divorce. The program recognizes that problems and disillusionment are normal in a marriage. However, many couples give up because they do not know what else to do.

Couples register for a three-hour session where a team of three alumni couples share their own experiences of disillusionment and the events and insights that created a spark of hope for them to attempt reconciliation. The new couples then consider their situation and how they are feeling about it. To aid in reaching a decision, a counselor will meet with the couple to help them tailor a plan to meet their needs. The reconciliation plan may include such things as counseling, meeting with a support group, programs for help in planning finances, parenting, and/or any other service which would be helpful.

ROH is based on sound psychological principles and basic spiritual values along with acceptance and support from volunteers and professionals. It provides a couple with time to review their marriage and make a decision about their future. While ROH is forthright in being "pro-marriage," it is most of all pro-health. Participants' decisions are honored and respected.

If you feel like giving up on your marriage, you may wish to contact the Recovery of Hope Network to find the center nearest you. Call (800) 327-2590.

Notes

Introduction
1. "How Common Is Pastoral Indiscretion?" *Leadership*, Vol. IX, No. 1, Winter 1988, 12.
2. Jerry B. Jenkins, *Hedges: Loving Your Marriage Enough to Protect It* (Brentwood, Tenn.: Wolgemuth & Hyatt, Publishers, Inc., 1989), 2.

Chapter 4
1. Jerry B. Jenkins, *Hedges: Loving Your Marriage Enough to Protect It* (Brentwood, Tenn.: Wolgemuth & Hyatt, Publishers, Inc., 1989).

Other Living Books Best-sellers

400 CREATIVE WAYS TO SAY I LOVE YOU by Alice Chapin. Perhaps the flame of love has almost died in your marriage, or you have a good marriage that just needs a little spark. Here is a book of creative, practical ideas for the woman who wants to show the man in her life that she cares. 07-0919-5

ANSWERS by Josh McDowell and Don Stewart. In a question-and-answer format, the authors tackle sixty-five of the most-asked questions about the Bible, God, Jesus Christ, miracles, other religions, and Creation. 07-0021-X

BUILDING YOUR SELF-IMAGE by Josh McDowell and Don Stewart. Here are practical answers to help you overcome your fears, anxieties, and lack of self-confidence. Learn how God's higher image of who you are can take root in your heart and mind. 07-1395-8

CHRISTIANITY: THE FAITH THAT MAKES SENSE by Dennis McCallum. Ideal for new teachers and group study, this readable apologetic presents a clear, rational defense for Christianity to those unfamiliar with the Bible and challenges readers to meet Christ personally. 07-0525-4

COME BEFORE WINTER AND SHARE MY HOPE by Charles R. Swindoll. A collection of brief vignettes offering hope and the assurance that adversity and despair are temporary setbacks we can overcome! 07-0477-0

DAWN OF THE MORNING by Grace Livingston Hill. Dawn Rensselaer is a runaway bride, fleeing a man she was tricked into marrying. But is she also running away from love? 07-0530-0

DR. DOBSON ANSWERS YOUR QUESTIONS by Dr. James Dobson. In this convenient reference book, renowned author Dr. James Dobson addresses heartfelt concerns on many topics, including marital relationships, infant care, child discipline, home management, and others. 07-0580-7

DR. DOBSON ANSWERS YOUR QUESTIONS: RAISING CHILDREN by Dr. James Dobson. A renowned authority on child-rearing offers his expertise on the spiritual training of children, sex education, discipline, coping with adolescence, and more. 07-1104-1

Other Living Books Best-sellers

FOR MEN ONLY edited by J. Allan Petersen. This book deals with topics of concern to every man: the business world, marriage, fathering, spiritual goals, and problems of living as a Christian in a secular world. 07-0892-X

GIVERS, TAKERS, AND OTHER KINDS OF LOVERS by Josh McDowell and Paul Lewis. Bypassing generalities about love and sex, this book answers the basics: Whatever happened to sexual freedom? Do men respond differently than women? Here are straight answers about God's plan for love and sexuality. 07-1031-2

HINDS' FEET ON HIGH PLACES by Hannah Hurnard. A classic allegory of a journey toward faith that has sold more than a million copies! 07-1429-6

LET ME BE A WOMAN by Elisabeth Elliot. This best-selling author combines her observations and experiences in a number of essays on male-female relationships. 07-2162-4

THE SEARCH FOR THE TWELVE APOSTLES by William Steuart McBirnie. Through travel, Bible study, and research, McBirnie has uncovered the history of Christ's apostles and their evangelical activities. The dedication and zeal of these men will inspire the faith of every reader. 07-5839-0

THE STRONG-WILLED CHILD by Dr. James Dobson. With practical solutions and humorous anecdotes, Dobson shows how to discipline an assertive child without breaking his spirit. Parents will learn to overcome feelings of defeat or frustration by setting boundaries and taking action. 07-5924-9

THROUGH GATES OF SPLENDOR by Elisabeth Elliot. This unforgettable story of five men who braved the Auca Indians has become one of the most famous missionary books of all time. 07-7151-6